# MAKE MONEY!
# DO YARD WORK

**Bridget Heos** | **Illustrated by Daniele Fabbri**

Amicus Illustrated is published by Amicus
P.O. Box 1329, Mankato, MN 56002
www.amicuspublishing.us

Library of Congress Cataloging-in-Publication Data
Heos, Bridget.
 Make money! Do yard work / by Bridget Heos;
illustrated by Daniele Fabbri.
   pages cm — (Make money!)
 Audience: K to grade 3.
 Summary: "Through trial and error and a few
humorous mistakes, a boy learns how to do simple
outside chores, get repeat customers, and create a
successful yard work business to earn enough money
to buy a digital music player" — Provided by publisher.
 ISBN 978-1-60753-363-4 (library binding) – ISBN
978-1-60753-411-2 (ebook)
1. Lawn care industry–Vocational guidance—Juvenile
literature. I. Fabbri, Daniele, 1978- illustrator. II. Title.
 SB433.27.H46 2014
 658'.041–dc23
                        2012050705

Editor: Rebecca Glaser
Designer: The Design Lab

Printed in the United States of America at
Corporate Graphics in North Mankato, Minnesota.

Date 11/2013  PO 1182

10 9 8 7 6 5 4 3 2

You want a really nice MP3 player? You only have $10 saved up. How could you ever earn $100?

Keeping a yard looking nice is hard work.
And hard work equals hard cash. Cha ching!

It's spring. You could plant flowers. How much should you charge? About $5 per hour seems fair. Check with your parents.

How will people know you're available? You could work in your own yard and hope the neighbors notice.

But you'll probably need to knock on some doors.

Well, good try.

Wait. There are other people on this block. What if you had a flyer to advertise your services?

Keep knocking on doors. If people aren't home, leave a flyer.

Your first customer! Mrs. Garza needs marigolds and petunias planted. She has the flowers and potting soil. You'll need a hand trowel and gardening gloves. They cost $10 at the hardware store.

Where should you plant the flowers?

Mrs. Garza says the flowers that need full sun go in the flower boxes. The flowers that need partial sun go in the pots.

Which is which? Oh look. It tells on these little signs. Good problem solving!

The flowers are planted. Now what? Time to collect your money.

Wait. Who will clean this up? That's your job, too. You also need to water the flowers. That's part of planting.

*Now* you can get paid. Your first $10!

You did a good job, so your neighbor told her friends. This is called word-of-mouth advertising. In June, you get three more jobs, and earn $30.

You still need money for the MP3 player. You could offer to plant more flowers—in places they've never thought of.

But that's not what your customers need. What *do* they need? How about weeding and watering their flowers? You can offer new services, or diversify.

In July, you find two customers who want you to weed their flower gardens every week. Be sure to find out which ones are weeds!

At $5 per garden, you'll earn $10 per week. There are 6 weeks left of summer, so you'll get $60 total for weeding.

You did it! You've earned $100, and you can buy the MP3 player. But it's fall, and some of your customers would like you to rake their yards. You could earn $15 per yard, and start saving for college.

Congratulations. You now have a year round business. And plenty of time to listen to music!

# Counting Your Money!

If you start doing yard work, keep track of how much you spend and how much you make. Here's a sample based on this story.

| | |
|---|---|
| BEGINNING SAVINGS | $10.00 |
| Buy trowel and gardening gloves | − 10.00 |
| You have left | 0.00 |
| | |
| MAY | |
| Plant flowers—Ms. Garza | $10.00 |
| | |
| JUNE | |
| Plant flowers—3 new customers | $30.00 |
| | |
| JULY | |
| Weed and Water week 1 | $10.00 |
| Weed and Water week 2 | $10.00 |
| | |
| AUGUST | |
| Weed and Water week 3 | $10.00 |
| Weed and Water week 4 | $10.00 |
| Weed and Water week 5 | $10.00 |
| Weed and Water week 6 | $10.00 |
| Total savings at end of summer | $100.00 |

# Glossary

**advertise** To tell customers about your business through signs or other messages.

**customer** A person who buys what you sell or pays for your services.

**diversify** To offer additional goods or services so that when business is slow in one area, you'll still have work in the other area.

**flyer** A piece of paper sharing information, such as about a business.

**problem solving** Figuring out the answer to a question by observing and thinking.

**word-of-mouth advertising** Customers telling others that they are happy with your goods or services.

# Read More

Antill, Sara. *10 Ways I Can Earn Money*. New York: PowerKids Press, 2012.

Orr, Tamra. *A Kid's Guide to Earning Money*. Hockessin, Del.: Mitchell Lane, 2009.

Scheunemann, Pam. *Cool Jobs for Yard-working Kids: Ways to Make Money Doing Yard Work*. Edina: Checkerboard, 2011.

# Websites

**It's My Life: Money**
*http://pbskids.org/itsmylife/money/*
Learn how to earn, save, and spend wisely.

**Money for Kids: Making Money**
*http://www.kidsmoney.org/makemone.htm*
Read advice from other kids who have tried earning money.

**My First Garden: A Guide to the World of Fun & Clever Gardening**
*http://urbanext.illinois.edu/firstgarden/*
Learn about how to choose a garden spot, the tools and supplies you'll need, and much more.

# About the Author

Bridget Heos is the author of more than 30 books for children, but made her millions babysitting in grade school and high school. She once babysat for a parrot who loved watching T.V. He would say, "Turn on Nick at Nite!" Visit her online at www.authorbridgetheos.com.

# About the Illustrator

Daniele Fabbri was born in Ravenna, Italy, in 1978. He graduated from Istituto Europeo di Design in Milan, Italy, and started his career as cartoon animator, storyboarder, and background designer for animated series. He has worked as a freelance illustrator since 2003, collaborating with international publishers and advertising agencies.